Napoleon in Russia

The Grand Army that Napoleon assembled for the invasion of Russia in June 1812 was half a million strong—the biggest fighting force the world had ever seen. Six months later, scarcely one in ten of those men remained alive. Thousands had died in battle, and many more of cold, hunger and disease. Napoleon had reached Moscow in triumph, but had been forced to retreat in panic through the bitter Russian winter. In two years, Napoleon's reign as Emperor of the French would be over.

Where had the great general gone wrong? In this fascinating book, Matthew Holden explains how he underestimated the strength of the Russians and allowed his army to be trapped in a hopeless position. He tells vividly how the Grand Army slowly melted away, as the frozen, starving soldiers dropped dead by the wayside on the endless march across the snow-covered plains. Finally he describes in detail the appalling climax, when the unarmed French camp-followers were cut to pieces by the Cossacks on the banks of the River Berezina.

MATTHEW HOLDEN obtained his M.A. degree in War Studies at the University of London; after a career as a newspaper War Correspondent, he now writes full-time on military subjects. His books include *The Legions of Rome, War in the Trenches, The Crusades* and *The Desert Rats* in the Sentinel series.

A WAYLAND SENTINEL BOOK

Napoleon in Russia

Matthew Holden

"Napoleon is like a stormy torrent which we cannot stop.
Moscow will be the sponge that sucks him in."
Field Marshal Kutusov explaining his strategy.

More Sentinel Books

Frontispiece: Napoleon watches his army cross the River Niemen on the march into Russia.

SBN 85340 396 1

© 1974 by Wayland (Publishers) Ltd.,
49 Lansdowne Place, Hove, Sussex BN3 1HF
2nd Impression 1980
Printed in Gt. Britain by
Page Bros (Norwich) Ltd
Mile Cross Lane, Norwich

Contents

List of Illustrations

1. Seeds of destruction

In Berlin, the school gates opened for the children to stream home for their midday meal. Among them ran thirteen-year-old Ludwig Rellstab. As he raced over the cobbles with his friends he heard the tremendous news—the mighty French, implacable enemies of Germany, had been defeated. The massive army which had been collected from every corner of Europe, and which Napoleon Bonaparte, the Emperor of France, had led into Russia, had been totally destroyed—by the peasant Russians, and by the fierce weather of this terrible winter of 1812.

Within hours Ludwig Rellstab was able to see for himself the terrible extent and effects of this destruction. Survivors of the French Forces, remnants of the so-called "Grand Army", struggled through the Berlin streets; many years later, the fearful sight still remained stark in Ludwig's memory.

"One saw no guns," he wrote, "no cavalry, only suffering men crippled by frightful wounds, men with hands, arms, or feet either missing or else completely destroyed by frostbite. That the hand of God could strike so terribly—I trembled to believe my own eyes."

Ludwig gaped at the farm-carts which rumbled and groaned along the roads: each was filled with straw, upon which lay the casualties, horribly wounded. "The stench from these carts was frightful. The festering and maybe gangrenous wounds gave off a really pestilential vapour . . . All who witnessed such scenes shuddered."

Among those who had ridden so confidently into Russia six months before had been a young lieutenant. The story of this man, twenty-one-year-old Heinrich Vossler, is the story of the whole incredible

Deplorable State of the French Troops returning from Moscow.

1812 campaign—a tale of courage and cruelty, of shattered hopes and hideous ordeals in the snowy Russian wilderness. . . .

Above French troops straggle back from Russia, as their comrades drop dead by the wayside.

Europe at war

Heinrich Vossler spent his childhood in the town of Tuttlingen, in the German state of Wurttenberg. In those days, Germany consisted of many small states, the most important of which was Prussia, with its capital Berlin.

All his life, Heinrich had known nothing but war. The French Revolution of 1789 led to massive upheaval. The crowned heads of Europe tried to destroy this new anti-Royalist power, and the years saw a succession of battles, defeats, treaties and triumphs.

It was on this troubled tide that Napoleon Bonaparte swept to power. His brilliant military skills led the French to victory against the Italians in 1796, and the Austrians in 1797. On 9th November, 1799, Napoleon became dictator of France. In the following year he smashed the Austrians at the Battle of Marengo, and again in December, 1805, at Austerlitz. He slaughtered the Prussians at Jena and Auerstädt (1806), and then defeated the Russians in 1807.

But Napoleon could not subdue the whole of Europe, despite all his military victories. His enemies constantly recovered and regrouped. In 1809, he defeated the Austrians yet again at Wagram. But meanwhile, far to the south in the Spanish peninsula, the British were beginning to gnaw at his empire. And, in the north, Russia too looked threatening. Prussia remained outwardly quiet, and had even allied herself to Napoleon—but many Germans hated this alliance, and longed for a chance to turn against the French tyranny.

Ever since he could remember, Heinrich had heard tales of these gigantic battles and shifting fortunes of war. Most of the stories centred upon Napoleon Bonaparte. The Emperor, born in Corsica in 1769,

Above The Emperor Napoleon in army uniform, by his court painter Horace Vernet.

was indeed a fantastic figure—a hero and a god, or a monster and a devil, according to whose side you were on.

Heinrich had seen drawings of him—he was about five feet six inches tall, with a broad chest covering enormously powerful lungs. These gave him tremendous energy. Napoleon was always on the move, and talked more or less non-stop. His face was pale and he had large, bluish-grey eyes.

Napoleon was neat in dress and behaviour. He loved long hot baths and hated bad smells—he found it an ordeal to stay in a room which had been freshly painted. He liked to rub his delicate hands with almond paste, and he had his hair cut once a week; he also sprinkled his head each day with light perfume.

But he was tough and tempestuous, too. Heinrich had heard of his sudden rages—Napoleon had been known to slap a general full in the face on the battlefield. Yet he usually seemed icy calm—so cool that he could curl up in his cloak and fall asleep when he wanted, even though cannons were thundering a few yards away.

Napoleon needed all his abilities now as he prepared to march into Russia. Soon those cannons would roar louder than ever before. And alongside the legendary leader Heinrich Vossler would fight, in his first and last campaign.

Left Napoleon gives orders to his troops on the battlefield of Jena.

The Grand Army

Even though he had defeated them six years before, many Germans still wanted to fight alongside Napoleon. Hundreds agreed with Heinrich when he said: "It was the hope of rapid promotion and a thirst for adventure which made me long for a war."

Adventurers like him flocked in their thousands to join the French army—the Grand Army. Never before had such a force been gathered. Fewer than half the soldiers were actually Frenchmen—the rest were Germans, Austrians, Poles, Italians, Dutch, Danes, Portuguese and Spaniards.

As many as 530,000 men marched or rode with Napoleon. Some merely sought excitement, or the spoils of war. Others were hardened professionals who had fought under Napoleon at Austerlitz, Jena and Auerstädt. These included men of the famous Imperial Guard, 36,000-strong, upon whom Napoleon relied for personal protection, and for the fiercest fighting. They had proud carved eagles for their standards, and wore tall bearskins on their heads.

Other soldiers were conscripts—forced to fight by the government of their country. In peacetime they might be university students, clerks, shop assistants, farmers. Most were reluctant to leave home. Many had very little military training, and they would be the first to die in battle. Usually they served as foot-soldiers. They would be ordered to charge on foot

Below Napoleon (on foot, centre) talks with an officer as the French army crosses the River Danube.

towards the enemy lines, perhaps directly at the
enemy guns—hence their nickname, "cannon-
fodder." Other infantrymen were more highly
trained. These included the *voltigeurs*, who like the
carabiniers were called light infantry—instead of
fighting in rigid lines, they were sent swarming across
the battlefield to exploit any enemy mistake.

Far more glamorous were the cavalrymen. These
might be *chasseurs* or hussars (light cavalry), or else
dragoons for the heavy shock tactics. They wore rich
colourful uniforms, with tight-fitting breeches and
plumed helmets, and huge whiskers on their faces.

About a quarter of the men in the Grand Army
were never intended to fight. They were the bridge-
builders, road engineers, cooks, grooms, servants,
surgeons and, most important, the commissariat
officers, whose job was to find food and supplies for
this vast host—these men would have the hardest task
of all.

Now, in the spring of 1812, the Grand Army began
to assemble in Poland ready for the advance into
Russia. From north, south and west, regiments began
to draw together. The coming campaign became the
sole topic of conversation in all the capitals of Europe.
Roads everywhere were blocked with carriages, guns
and marching columns of men.

Many of the soldiers were unaware who the enemy
would be—some thought they were about to advance
south towards Italy. But, on the far side of Poland, the
Russians were also preparing for gigantic conflict.

Left Napoleon reviews soldiers
of the Grand Army before the
invasion of Russia.

13

The army of the Tsar

Napoleon's troops outnumbered the Russians, who had only about 427,000 men under arms, half of them scattered through the west and centre of the country. But the Russians were to prove worthy opponents for the Grand Army.

Most Russian soldiers came from peasant stock, and were used to living an almost slave-like existence. Troops were forced to fight for a period of twenty-five years, and once they were conscripted, their families never expected to see them again. Newcomers to the ranks had their heads shaved clean, as a sign of military service.

But these men were extremely tough and fit. Officials were very careful whom they chose for the army—they did not hesitate to reject men for such minor defects as bad teeth. And the recruits made excellent infantrymen. One British observer explained why: the Russian peasants were used to "extremes of weather and hardship, to the worst and scantiest food, to marches for days and nights, of four hours' repose and six hours' progress; accustomed to hard work and to carrying heavy loads; ferocious, but disciplined; obstinately brave, and ... devoted to their sovereign, their chief, and their country."

Their sovereign at this time was Tsar Alexander I, ruler of Russia since his father had been murdered in 1801. Alexander was gentle, handsome and courteous, capable of inspiring intense devotion in his subjects. But Alexander had his faults. He would start things with boundless enthusiasm, but left unfinished almost everything he did: he started to read books, yet rarely reached the last page. His military knowledge was just sufficient to enable him to argue

Below An English cartoon showing Tsar Alexander I putting out Napoleon's candle.

14

with his generals, but he lacked the confidence and skill to take command himself.

The most important of Alexander's generals was Mikhail Barclay de Tolly, born in 1761 to a family of Scottish immigrants. Barclay was a strange character. He began his military service in the ranks, and worked his way up to the supreme command. But he lacked the strength to deal with the interfering Alexander. Nor would he stand by his own convictions in the face of high-born officers, who sneered at his humble beginnings.

This same mixture of good and bad could be found among the Russian officers as a whole. They delighted in the glory of war and dressed in sumptuous uniforms. They were capable of tremendous physical effort and acted with extreme courage. Yet they loved to gamble and drink, and spent long hours over their food—after which they preferred to take naps rather than fight.

The Russian army in the spring of 1812 remained full of confidence. The French had beaten them before, but this had been some years ago, in 1805–07. They believed they had learned the correct lessons from these mistakes. Above all, the Russians were defending their sacred homeland. And what better cause could they have than that?

Weapons at War

Both armies used the same types of weapons. They were all designed to inflict the greatest pain and mutilation upon the enemy, while giving maximum protection to the user.

Most infantrymen, who formed the bulk of these armies, were armed with muskets. These cumbersome weapons could not be relied upon to kill a man if he were more than 250 yards away. Indeed, they proved so inaccurate that even at half this range it was hardly worth aiming at a particular person.

Instead, infantrymen fired together *en masse*. Each man loaded, raised and fired his musket at the same time, so that as many musket balls as possible scythed through the enemy ranks. But so difficult were these weapons to load that only two volleys could be discharged a minute. In the meantime the cavalry would try to swoop in, or the enemy infantry would try to charge forward and destroy the opposing line with their bayonets.

Yet when musket volleys were fired the effect could be devastating. The soft bullets mushroomed out when they hit the bodies, lifting men from their feet with the impact and inflicting ghastly funnel-shaped wounds.

Equally terrible were the cavalry charges, especially those of the heavy cavalry—*cuirassiers* or dragoons. Most horsemen were armed with sabres, either designed for slashing downwards with razor-sharp cutting edges, or for jabbing, in which case their points were especially sharp.

Even more deadly were the *uhlans* or lancers. These cavalrymen, armed with light steel-tipped wooden lances, could unseat or spit an enemy cavalryman, or

Below A ten-pound cannon used by the Russians in 1812, now in an open-air museum on the site of the Battle of Borodino.

16

they could play havoc with enemy infantry while staying beyond the range of the foot-soldiers' bayonets.

But by far the worst casualties were caused by the massive artillery bombardments, with which Napoleon displayed his greatest skill. Infantrymen had to stand in rigid lines, both to let their officers control them better, and also to fire heavier volleys. Unfortunately, these lines made them sitting targets for enemy cannon. Three kinds of missiles were hurled by the artillery: round-shot, shells, and case. Round-shot consisted of solid iron balls which sliced through bone and flesh. Even when these balls were rolling on the ground at the end of their runs they could still rip off a man's leg.

Shells were lighter and less capable of rolling: if they failed to explode in flight they lay spluttering until the fuse burned down. Case-shot, also known as cannister or grape, was used for short ranges: containers were packed tight with musket balls, iron scraps or even horse-shoe nails and the bag burst to spew the contents into the enemy ranks.

Above The wide variety of uniforms worn by soldiers in the French army. By the end of the Russian campaign, they were wearing whatever rags they could find.

17

Battle and aftermath

Such battles became a gigantic milling mass of men and horses, all embroiled in a hellish and apparently chaotic upheaval. From start to finish the shattering din would continue, and the whole area would be covered by thick choking smoke.

Each side tried to batter the other to death: through musket volleys, artillery salvoes or cavalry charges. It is easy to imagine these cavalry attacks: long lines of horsemen thundering down upon the enemy, horses at full gallop. But such a picture is not entirely correct. In reality the charges were made over short distances, probably no more than 250 yards. The horsemen would start at a trot, then increase to a canter. Only in the last fifty yards or so would they open out into a gallop. And at the end of a hard day's battle the attack might be made at little more than a walk.

Infantrymen defended themselves by forming squares, to give protection from all directions: each side of the square consisted of three or more ranks, with guns at the corners. Cavalrymen could do little against well-disciplined squares: musket volleys could be most effective, and, at shorter range, the upward-sloping bayonets faced the horsemen with a deadly forest of steel.

But unfortunately these squares made excellent targets for the artillery. The guns would first blast away at them, then, if the square crumbled, the cavalry would charge in. Experienced infantrymen would hurl themselves flat if this happened and the square could no longer give protection: if they lay on the ground the cavalrymen could not always reach low enough to slash them with their sabres, and horses shy from treading on living bodies.

Yet within an hour or two the battlefield would be heaped with corpses and mangled men. The wounded had little chance of survival: medical surgery was primitive then. Chest or stomach wounds were crudely stitched up or plastered over, regardless of any damage inside the wound. Bare fingers probed in the blood to look for embedded missiles.

Surgery meant amputation and little else. There was no time for cleaning and treating shattered arms or legs. Anyway, the time would probably be wasted: round shot and sabre thrusts caused such terrible internal damage that only drastic treatment would do. So the limbs were simply sawn off—without antiseptics or anaesthetics. The men remained fully conscious, and had to be forcibly held down on the tables: wine and diluted rum were used to strengthen patients before an operation, not to render them insensible.

Never would the list of casualties be more colossal or the battles more bloody than in this fearful campaign of 1812.

Above French infantry resist an Austrian cavalry charge at the Battle of Fleurus.

2. Advance

Why should Napoleon Bonaparte wish to unleash this horror? He had no desire to conquer Russia. Indeed, his character was by no means as warlike as might be supposed. His primary reason stemmed not from ambition, but from fear.

Napoleon had land enough, and wished above all to rebuild France. He had exciting plans for reorganizing Government, for new buildings, for reforming education—he spent more money on schools than on anything else—and he took a close interest in the country's taxation system. He once spotted a tiny error of 1 franc 45 cents in a huge ministerial budget.

The Emperor of France, one of the greatest military leaders the world has known, was tired of war. He showed more interest in matters of peace. Even four years earlier, while fighting the British in Spain, he had written to his Minister of the Interior in Paris: "I see from the papers that you have laid the foundation-stone of the fountain on the site of the Bastille. I assume that the stone elephant will stand in the centre of a huge basin filled with water, that it will be a handsome beast, and big enough for people to be able to get inside . . ."

Moreover, Napoleon had a high regard for the Russian leader, Tsar Alexander. "Were he a woman," he had admitted. "I think I should fall passionately in love with him."

But Napoleon's very desire for peace precipitated war. He wanted to make reforms in the Grand Duchy

Above The political situation in 1812—the Napoleonic monkey is threatened by the Russian bear and the British bulldog.

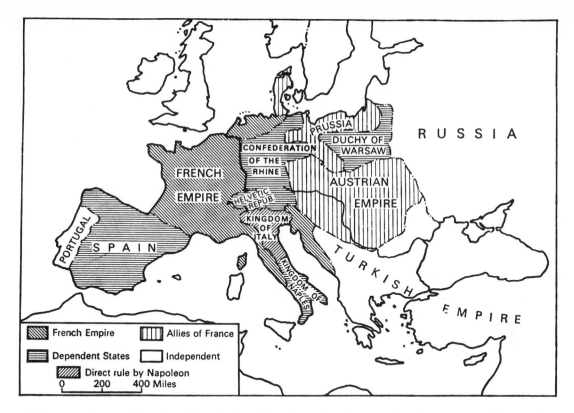

French Empire

Allies of France

Dependent States

Independent

Direct rule by Napoleon

0 200 400 Miles

of Warsaw (part of Poland) including freedom for the peasants and equal political rights for the Jews.

Alexander's advisers were horrified. All this on the border of Russian territory might give ideas to the Russian peasants. Napoleon must be stopped—and they urged the hesitant Tsar to adopt a hostile attitude: Napoleon must take his troops out of Prussia and the Grand Duchy, or there would be trouble.

Napoleon, reluctant to start a war, was also reluctant to give back territory—which he feared the Russians would immediately seize and use to threaten France. He also believed that the Poles wanted to stay within his Empire.

So he chose invasion. If he could defeat the Russians he might win time in which he could rebuild France and persuade the English to end the war. He knew the difficulties would be immense; but his Grand Army nevertheless began to assemble.

Above In 1812, Napoleon and his allies between them controlled most of Europe.

The army prepares

The young Heinrich Vossler reached Poland on 18th April. The countryside appalled him: so poor, so ugly, and the people so wretched.

"We began to move across the vast plain, disfigured here and there by villages whose houses resembled our pig-sties back at home." These were the homes of the people who, unknown to Heinrich, provided the immediate cause for the coming campaigns. If Napoleon had his way, he would change this poverty and slavery. But to do so, he would first have to defeat the Russian army.

Final preparations were yet to be completed. This was a monumental task. Thousands upon thousands of men had to be equipped and fed; the animals alone totalled 200,000, all of them needing fodder. No less than 26 transport battalions were formed for the Grand Army. Four of these were each given 600 light carts, four had heavy ox-drawn vehicles, while the rest were each equipped with 252 four-horse wagons.

Each regiment had its own bakers, masons, tailors, shoe-makers, gunsmiths, farriers and other craftsmen. The corps led by Marshal Louis-Nicolas Davoût seemed especially well-supplied. Every soldier was told to have the following in his knapsack: spare shirts, shoes, trousers, gaiters, cleaning and repair kit, bandages, lint and sixty rounds of ammunition. In addition, each man carried biscuits, flour and bread, and hand-grinders to mill local corn. Every day about a quarter of a million loaves of bread were needed (and so a million sacks of flour). During an average day's march, about 100,000 pairs of boots would be worn through and over 10,000 horses' hooves would have to be reshod.

French supply officers worked day and night to collect all these stores. And yet no matter how conscientious officers and commanders like Davoût might have been, the total equipment would still have fallen short. Napoleon knew this, and an eye-witness described his arrival at the main camp on 21st June:

"Despite its coating of dust, the Emperor's face showed signs of fatigue, excitement and displeasure caused by bad news he had received on the way. His ill-humour changed to anger when he learned . . . that not only the army but even the Guard was short of provisions. He did not sleep that night, and everywhere people were organizing ovens to bake bread."

Such a massive army, containing dozens of nationalities, would be very hard to control for a long period, and almost impossible to supply. Napoleon therefore hoped for a short campaign before his equipment and provisions ran out: otherwise his army would be like a stranded whale. Never before had Napoleon's campaigning plans been so important for the survival of his forces.

Below French soldiers dragging a cannon over rough ground where horses could not be used.

Plans for victory

Napoleon put his hopes on winning an early victory, which would make Tsar Alexander seek peace. He had no desire to advance deep into Russian territory, and had certainly no plan to capture either of its two capitals, Moscow or St. Petersburg.

He wanted to strike over the River Niemen into Russian-controlled East Poland, aiming to slash between the two main enemy armies led by Barclay and General Peter Ivanovich Bagration. The main French army would force Barclay back. A second French force under Marshal Jérôme would move against Bagration—although with less pressure, so that Bagration would not withdraw as quickly as Barclay, thus widening the gap between them.

With the Russians divided, Napoleon planned to encircle them and threaten their supply lines back into their homeland. Then each could be destroyed in turn. Napoleon's line of advance would be towards the city of Vilna: here, he hoped, the all-important battle with Barclay would be fought.

On 23rd June Napoleon rode forward to study the Niemen river, the natural frontier between Russian and French-occupied Poland. During the evening he briefed his commanders.

"Although the weather was very hot," wrote an eye-witness, "Napoleon kept on his dark overcoat and his little hat which he wore while talking to the generals and marshals, whereas these all stood uncovered to listen. He often walked round the office, and looked at the plans and maps as he gave out his orders . . . he was certainly in a very bad mood, because he dictated letters in a terrible tone of voice."

Napoleon's temper might have improved had he

known of discussions taking place in the enemy camp. Russian plans were pretty confused. General Barclay's army of some 127,000 men lay north of the Niemen, with its headquarters in the Vilna area. General Bagration lay to the south. The Russian leaders disagreed over the correct defence to be adopted: Barclay wanted a battle at Vilna—just as Napoleon did. But the Tsar, and his adviser General Ernst von Phull, wished to fall back on half-completed defensive positions at Drissa.

Napoleon might well take advantage of such arguments. And, soon after dawn on 24th June, the main part of the Grand Army began to surge across the Niemen near Kovno. Another column forded the river at Tilsit, eighty miles to the west, while a third crossed at Grodno, a similar distance south. Napoleon left about a fifth of his force behind to guard the frontier.

The historic campaign had begun. "From now on," wrote Heinrich Vossler, marching with one of the leading corps, "I was to witness and, indeed, experience, scenes of every imaginable distress, wretchedness and misery."

Opposite The two leading Russian generals at the start of the campaign: *top,* Prince Barclay de Tolly, and *bottom,* Peter Bagration.

Above Another impression (see *Frontispiece*) of Napoleon watching the Grand Army crossing the River Niemen.

25

Invasion

Regiment after regiment tramped across the specially built wooden bridges. Hundreds of hooves thudded on the planks, the cavalry harnesses jingling; gun carriages creaked. The bridges groaned beneath their weight. Drums beat a steady tattoo, with an endless throb which the enemy would soon come to know so well: *"Tum ti-ti-tum tum tum ti-ti-tum tum . . ."* Officers bawled commands at their troops, already sweating and cursing as their goat-skin knapsacks bit into their backs.

Napoleon stood on the river bank and watched his men flood over to the other side. He tapped his boot with his riding-crop. Behind him waited a detachment of the Imperial Guard, their belts and buckles glittering in the sun.

The morning had dawned bright. But by noon clouds began to gather in the east; the sky grew dark and the first large drops of rain began to fall. Men, still wet with sweat, began to shiver.

Black clouds boiled and thunder rumbled like distant gunfire. A fierce deluge drenched the advancing French columns late in the afternoon. Drums were unslung to prevent damage to the skins, the beating of rain on the soldiers' capes replacing the incessant tattoo. Muskets were carried upside down, to stop water running down into the barrels.

More and more regiments crossed the Niemen, making their way into the gently rolling countryside with its forests, lakes and marshes. In front rode the fantastic figure of Joachim Murat, King of Naples and commander of the advance guard. He wore huge gold spurs, massive riding boots and an elaborately embroidered jacket of light blue. Black ringlets cascaded

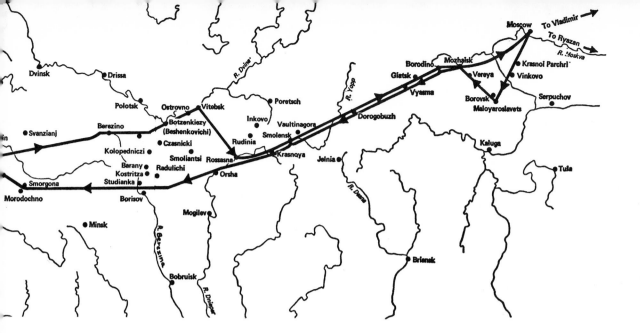

from beneath his white-feathered hat. An entire cart was needed to carry his perfumes and cosmetics. But Murat enjoyed a reputation as one of the finest cavalry leaders of his time.

Ahead, somewhere not too far away, lay the enemy; already Russian scouts had been reported, watching the invasion. Enemy patrols made off as soon as the French came too close.

Heinrich Vossler, marching in the midst of the Grand Army, wrote in his diary: "In two days and nights, during which each regiment and corps seemed to be treading on the heels of the other, the passage of the river was completed."

Despite the absence of enemy opposition, casualties were already being suffered. The sudden break in the weather caused heavy losses in horses and other livestock through sickness, and many troops fell ill. Moreover, the road became harder as the troops splashed through the puddles: supply wagons became bogged down in the mud. The storms, like the black crows perching on the fence-posts by the road, seemed a bad omen.

Above Map showing the route of Napoleon's march through Russia.

Opposite Joachim Murat in his marshal's uniform.

27

Russian reaction

Above Russian peasants defending their home against the invading French.

Russian scouts keeping watch at the Niemen reined round their horses as the first French began to cross towards them, and heeled their mounts back to the army headquarters. Within twenty-four hours of the French move forward, Tsar Alexander issued a ringing appeal to his people: "Warriors! You defend your religion, your country and your liberty. I am with you."

Despite these vigorous words, Russian plans were still in chaos. Word of the French invasion first reached the headquarters at Vilna on the evening of 24th June, while the Tsar and his staff were at a magnificent ball. The news created immediate uproar.

This panic destroyed General Barclay's last hopes of making a stand at Vilna. The headquarters began to pull back in confusion, initially to Svanziani. Alexander, and his adviser General Ernst von Phull, still hoped to use the defensive positions even further back at Drissa. They envisaged a stand by Barclay's First Army at this point, while Prince Bagration struck from the south with the Second Army to attack Napoleon on his flank.

But the arguments went on. Phull believed that Barclay was withdrawing too slowly, risking being surrounded by the advancing French. Indeed, the first enemy cavalrymen rode into Vilna just thirty minutes after the last Russian troops had left. Barclay, on the other hand, was still reluctant to give up Russian territory.

Others agreed with the army commander. "How terrible!" wailed Shishkov, the Tsar's secretary. "To lose Vilna only five days after the opening of hostilities! To run away, to abandon so many towns and so much territory to the enemy, and with all that, to boast of such a beginning! Oh, merciful Lord, my words are washed in bitter tears!''

Yet Napoleon was forced to wait at Vilna to settle urgent administrative problems and to let supplies catch up with the advance. This halt gave the Russians a short breathing space, and during this time Alexander inspected the defences at Drissa that General Phull was relying on. When he saw the inadequate half-finished fortifications, he was convinced at last that to make a stand here would be suicidal.

The Russians had only one other choice—to retreat further until a proper position could be found for battle. Moreover, a longer Russian withdrawal would allow Prince Bagration to move back towards Barclay. With their two forces united, the Russians would be in a far stronger situation.

Almost despite themselves, the Russians were thwarting Napoleon's plans and were adopting the best policy—to withdraw, lead on the French, and unite. Napoleon's hopes for a decisive battle early in the campaign, before his supply problems crippled him, would be smashed.

Below Soldiers of the Imperial Guard resting at an outpost near Vilna.

Road to Smolensk

Heinrich Vossler rode with the rest of the Grand Army into a deserted, brooding, silent landscape, sullen with dark forests and wide empty fields. From time to time enemy forces darted forward to snap at the advancing French, before turning and running again.

Especially adept at this harassment were the Cossacks. These wild horsemen spent most of their lives in the saddle and were ideally equipped for scouting and skirmishing. They wore practical clothes: tight blue jackets and wide blue trousers, and their favourite weapon was an eight-foot lance. They were soon to be feared throughout the French army.

To start with, the French invaders were in high spirits. The army seemed so strong that nothing could stand in its way. Then, very soon, Napoleon and his generals found that the enemy did not mean to block their progress after all. And supply difficulties increased with each mile.

The Grand Army was as big as a modern city such as Leeds or Edinburgh. And all the time this horde had to be kept on the move, along rough roads. Moreover, supplies had to be brought up from the rear and hurried many miles forward to reach the troops. This became even harder after the Russians began their "scorched earth" policy—stripping nearby fields and villages of supplies before the French arrived, burning the crops and polluting the water.

And already the French had another enemy: the fickle weather. Heinrich wrote: "We were embarked on a strenuous campaign entailing frequent forced marches along abominable roads, either smothered in sand or knee-deep in mud and frequently pitted by

precipitous gulleys, under skies alternatively unbearably hot or pouring forth freezing rain."

One French sergeant described the situation near Vilna: "The hailstorm was so bad that we had great trouble in controlling our horses, and it became necessary to tether them to the wheels. I was half dead with cold, and unable to stand it any longer I opened one of my wagons and took refuge inside. Next morning a heart-rending sight met our eyes. In the cavalry camp near by the ground was covered with horses which had died of cold. More than 10,000 perished during this night of horror." Losses this size are hard to imagine.

Napoleon still tried to cut between the two Russian armies led by General Barclay in the north and Prince Bagration in the south. But despite a successful French action at Mogilev on 23rd July, Bagration continued to withdraw eastwards across the River Dnieper. His line of march would take him towards Barclay at Smolensk: Napoleon staked his hopes on a battle at this important city. His commanders were ordered to urge their weary men forward at all possible speed.

Above Cossack cavalrymen pursue the retreating enemy while their women strip the valuables from a dead Frenchman.

Smolensk

So far the Grand Army had been moving through the Russian part of Poland. Now, at the Dvina River, the advance would proceed into the Russian homeland itself.

"I had crossed the Niemen in a state of tense expectation," wrote Lieutenant Vossler. "Now our move into enemy territory proper filled me with nothing but sombre forebodings ... Dense and menacing forests met the eye in every direction. The rare villages were deserted. Not a sign of human life anywhere. The fate of this huge army to which I belonged oppressed me profoundly."

Vossler's hands were raw from the rubbing reins. The heat remained intense; he had had to crouch with his men to drink water from filthy puddles. Hundreds of soldiers complained of stomach pains.

On 25th July the Russians began a three-day delaying action at Vitebsk. Then they pulled back again and the French moved on, over the strewn corpses of the fallen, bloated and stinking in the summer heat. Further clashes with the Russian rearguard took place, none of them serious.

At Vitebsk, Napoleon had to hold up his advance for two weeks. He had urgent diplomatic business to attend to, especially over the war in Spain. His supply system was still grossly deficient; his army had begun to display an increasing lack of unity.

On 1st August the two Russian armies under Barclay and Bagration joined forces near Smolensk, with Barclay as overall commander. But the Russians too were suffering: their soldiers and horses were short of food, and medical services for the wounded were crude. Some of the worst Vitebsk casualties received no treatment at all; on 6th August the Tsar was handed a report which declared: "Many of them arrived from Vitebsk unbandaged, because there were only two doctors. There is a complete shortage of medicines and bandages, and worms are eating many of the wounded alive."

Moreover, the Russians were still quarrelling over the correct plan of campaign. Barclay was still not sure whether to pull back further, or go into battle at Smolensk. Intense pressure was put on him, and, on 8th August, the commander reluctantly decided to fight.

He began to manoeuvre for position to the north of the city—only to scurry back to Smolensk on hearing that the French were now advancing rapidly this way. "Barclay was unsure at this moment," wrote one participant, "whether his own head stood on his shoulders." Only about 15,000 Russian troops were to stay in the city, to keep the French at bay while important magazines of ammunition were cleared out; after this Barclay would continue the retreat.

Napoleon, on the other hand, sought his decisive battle. Cavalrymen were thrown forward to outflank and trap the enemy. His half-starved, weary troops were hurried down the narrow, dusty roads towards the city.

Below Napoleon confers with his marshals on a hilltop overlooking the battlefield at Smolensk.

Battle—and retreat

Around Smolensk lay an ancient brick wall, about thirty feet high and fifteen feet thick at the base, studded with fortifications. In front stretched a ditch: soon this would be heaped with dead.

At six o'clock in the morning, 16th August, the French bombardment of the city began. Shells screamed into the houses; crashing masonry echoed the roar of the guns; so close were the salvoes that the whole sky hung thick with smoke. The Russian defenders struggled like rats from the rubble and carved out fresh defensive positions from the ruins of the houses.

Hour after hour the cannonade went on from the shimmering hills outside Smolensk. The sweating gunners, blackened with gunpowder, pumped shell after shell into the smoking city. And, under cover of the tremendous battering, lines of French infantry swept towards the city walls, their crackling musket fire sounding sharp amidst the artillery tumult.

Wave after wave of French foot-soldiers curled around the walls, only to be broken and sent reeling back by the desperate defenders. The wounded tried to drag themselves across the open to safety, or lay moaning for water beneath the overpowering sun.

Throughout the day the battle raged. General Barclay fed more troops into the city during the evening; fighting went on next day. For almost thirteen hours the Russians endured a massive artillery bombardment: many were buried alive, blown to pieces, or permanently deafened by the ear-splitting noise.

But gradually the Russians were pounded from the outskirts. Bloody street fighting went on into the night, illuminated by the ghastly glow of burning houses.

Napoleon watched this huge flickering fire from the near-by slopes. One thing he knew—no city could withstand such punishment.

"It's an eruption of Vesuvius," he shouted to an *aide-de-camp*. "It's a fine sight, is it not?"

"**It's** horrible, sir."

"Bah!" snapped Napoleon. "Gentlemen, remember the words of a Roman emperor: 'The corpse of an enemy always smells sweet'."

But Napoleon had still been denied the decisive battle which he needed so badly. In the middle of the night the Russian guns suddenly fell deathly silent. Soon there came a sky-rending explosion: the last of the ammunition in the stores had been deliberately blown up. General Barclay issued the order to withdraw.

The exhausted, filthy survivors slipped away from the ruins of the city to join the main army, and the Russians resumed the retreat. More than six thousand Russians had been slaughtered—but Napoleon had probably lost about eight thousand. At daybreak on 18th August the French took possession of Smolensk. But it was to prove a bitter victory.

Below A scene in the Russian camp during the battle at Smolensk.

Bitter victory

Above Vasilisa Kozhina, the leader of a band of guerillas who repeatedly attacked stragglers from the French army.

Lieutenant Vossler stayed outside the city, and so was spared the terrible sights which sickened his comrades when they crept into the streets. They found black smoking ruins—and piles of charred and broken bodies.

"The burning suburbs," wrote one Frenchman, "the dense multi-coloured smoke, the red glow, the crash of exploding shells, the thunder of cannon, the rattling rifle-fire, the beating of drums, the moans and groans of old men, women and children, the whole people falling on their knees with arms outstretched to the skies—such was the picture that greeted our eyes and tore at our hearts."

In some places the Russians had been unable to evacuate the wounded before the fire spread. "These unfortunates, abandoned to a cruel death, lay here in piles, charred, almost without human form, among the smoking ruins and flaming beams. The position of many corpses showed the ghastly torments that must have preceded death."

Yet the main Russian army had pulled away. Napoleon pushed his men on. "Within a month," he declared, "we shall be in Moscow. In six weeks we shall have peace." The Emperor had realized that he must strike for the capital itself: no longer could he hope for a decisive battle near the frontier.

He tried once again to encircle the Russians near Valutino Gora, five miles east of Smolensk, on 19th August. Fighting lasted throughout the day, and troops under Marshal Ney eventually forced the Russians to abandon their positions. But an out-flanking movement by André Junot came too late, and too weakly, and Barclay pulled back from the

trap. Junot's timid attempt led to his disgrace; he lost his sanity a few months later.

Meantime Napoleon had lost another seven thousand men, more than the Russians. Daily, the tortures of the advance multiplied. Food became even more scarce.

"The heat was extreme," wrote one young Captain. "Furious gusts of wind swirled up such dense clouds of dust that often we could no longer see the great trees which lined the road. The sacred soil of Russia which we were invading seemed, in obedience to the summons by the young fanatics of Smolensk, to rise against the invaders."

The horses of the Grand Army had to be fed on green fodder because there was no hay to be had, and this led to extensive sickness. "After a hard ride they succumbed in their hundreds," observed Heinrich Vossler. "We found them lying by the roadside in droves." He added, "The sight of them much increased our forebodings about the state of the Grand Army's cavalry and artillery."

Unknown to Heinrich, the French would soon need every available horse and all the strength they could muster. The greatest and bloodiest battle of the 1812 campaign, and perhaps of the whole Napoleonic era, lay just ahead.

Above A Russian council of war during the retreat towards Moscow. Field Marshal Kutusov (seated, left) is explaining his tactics to his officers.

Back to Borodino

Above Field Marshal Mikhail Kutusov, architect of the Russian strategy of retreat.

The Russians faced grave problems too. Arguments still went on over the correct plan to adopt, and in the second capital of St. Petersburg increasing panic afflicted the leading citizens.

General Barclay could still not make up his mind. He continued to survey ground for a possible battle, but with reluctance. His rival, the haughty Prince Bagration, demanded greater efforts. Yet the Russian army still stumbled back—which, in fact, was still the best thing for it to do.

At the end of August Tsar Alexander decided he must appoint a new supreme commander for his armies. Barclay would henceforth only control the First Army: in his place General Mikhail Kutusov was summoned to the front.

One-eyed and aged sixty-seven, Kutusov proved an extremely cunning warrior. He disliked the Tsar, and the feeling was returned, but Alexander knew of no better choice. The new commander was determined to outwit Napoleon, and he wanted an all-out battle even less than Barclay. He knew he would be obliged to fight one, because of the pressures from St. Petersburg, but he nevertheless realized that the best hope for salvation would be to tempt the enemy deep inside Russia.

And so the retreat went on, with Kutusov making soothing sounds to reassure the citizens in the capital. He heard with satisfaction the reports of French suffering. The sun still scorched the Grand Army; French soldiers fought among themselves for a gulp of brackish swamp water. The Cossacks circled vulture-like to pick off stragglers; more and more soldiers and horses died on the dusty road. The days were filled with the sound of muskets snapping in the background, and occasionally cannon, and always the pall of black smoke hung over deserted and destroyed villages.

Then, on the morning of 3rd September, the Russian army marched from the Kolotskoi Monastery to the little valleys and low rounded hills encircling the village of Borodino. And here Kutusov halted; this would be his battlefield. Moscow lay only seventy miles away.

Napoleon, too, called a halt and began to prepare. His spirits rose, and so did those of his soldiers: at last the Russians could be made to fight, and defeated. Heinrich Vossler described the French camp on 6th September. "The whole army seemed alive with a cheerful bustle, and if one discounted the pale, worn faces of the soldiers he could fancy himself in a camp replete to the point of abundance. Most of the troops were busily polishing and repairing weapons for the morrow, and the order reached us to make an early night of it so as to be ready for the morning's work. Many a soldier stretched himself out carefree and contented, little thinking that this would be his last night on earth . . ."

Below Napoleon with officers and men of the Imperial Guard on the heights above Borodino.

Borodino—the beginning

Above Part of the vast battlefield at Borodino, seen from Napoleon's headquarters.

So weak had Heinrich Vossler become during the long march that he could barely mount his horse unaided. His tattered clothes hung from his lice-bitten frame: his hair had begun to fall out, and his teeth felt loose in their blackened sockets.

"A miserable plateful of bread soup oiled with the stump of a tallow candle was all that I had to eat on the eve of the big battle. But in my famished condition even this revolting dish seemed quite appetizing. I ate it gratefully, laid down to rest and slept, like the others, as peacefully as if the coming day was to have resembled its fellows as one egg does another."

During the evening Napoleon tried to hearten his men by making a stirring announcement: "Let them say of you: he was in the great battle under the walls of Moscow!" Yet the Emporer slept uneasily in his tent, anxious lest the Russians should steal away again: during the night be constantly asked if the enemy camp fires still lit the slopes opposite.

Napoleon had decided to make a direct frontal assault on the Russian positions, despite the enormous casualties which would result. To work round the Russian line would take time, during which the enemy might once more escape.

Dawn began to streak the sky at five o'clock on 7th September. Thirty minutes later the sun crept up red behind the Russian defences. Napoleon, suffering from stomach pains and a cold, had risen at first light. His Grand Army had already been severely reduced in numbers: he now had just over 120,000 men for the Battle of Borodino—other regiments would not be able to arrive in time. Russian strength would be roughly the same.

And now the two armies were standing to arms. The two lines were only a few hundred yards apart, and each could hear murmurings and shouted commands from each other.

Napoleon rode slowly to his command post, slightly to the right of the French centre. An officer rushed forward to give him a chair. Napoleon turned round and sat astride it with his arms resting on the back. Raising his telescope he peered at the scene before him.

Over in the Russian lines the generals were issuing last-minute instructions. The men waited tense in their fortified positions, especially at the main earthworks in the centre, known as the Great Redoubt and the most likely point for the fiercest fighting.

Suddenly a flash was seen to the left and a cannon shot boomed out. Two more followed, then came a slight pause. And then hundreds of cannon thundered with an abrupt earth-trembling roar. The Battle of Borodino had begun.

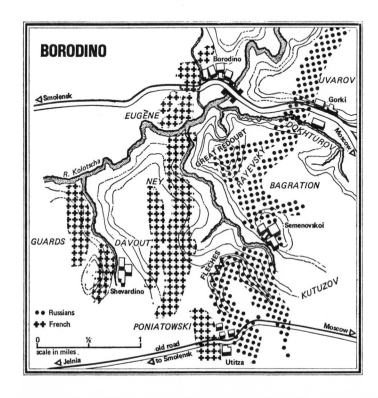

Borodino—noon

"The thunder of artillery came from all sides," wrote Lieutenant Vossler, "at times even drowning the rattle of musketry. We formed up, and began our advance."

Repeated shouts sent thick swarms of infantrymen walking towards the Russian lines, Vossler among them. He could see no further than the man in front; the men gripped their muskets tight. On either side explosions erupted, with earth and bodies hurled up to the sky, as Russian shells tore bloody holes in the advancing French.

"Soon we found ourselves subjected to a veritable hail of grapeshot," wrote Vossler. Then musket volleys ripped into the French ranks, slaughtering scores at each delivery. But the first troops in Heinrich's regiment had reached the enemy and were running forward with their bayonets, screaming as they charged.

"There was nothing for it but to advance as rapidly as we could. Now the enemy cavalry launched a series of attacks, but we stood our ground, while on either side the infantry struggled in fearful carnage."

Henrich Vossler and his men hurried into a square formation, stumbling over mounting heaps of bodies. Masses of Russian cavalrymen stabbed at the square, but the formation held. Other regiments came through the smoke to give support and the advance plunged forward again.

But now Heinrich would be spared further ordeal. "A captain at my side was wounded and almost at the same moment I was hit by a richochet on the brass band of my helmet and knocked unconscious." Men dragged him to the rear.

More than half of Heinrich's regiment had been killed or wounded. The same happened at all points in the battlefield. Positions were taken and re-taken; soldiers used the piled bodies of their comrades for protection. Trenches overflowed with dead, especially at the Great Redoubt. The whole smoking battlefield was now one vast surging mass of men and horses, locked in mortal combat.

Russian troops ran forward to bayonet the onrushing French, lunging to cut open the bellies of the horses, dragging men down from their saddles, screaming as they stabbed in frenzy. But still the French came on, and still the artillery pounded the defences. French cavalry charges were so close to one another that there seemed to be just one solid thrust. Horses whose riders had been shot down ran wildly about.

Amidst this carnage were many extraordinary incidents. One Russian officer, trying to attract his commander's attention, had an upraised arm torn off by a cannonball. Thrown from his horse he raised his other arm, still trying to gain his General's attention.

Barclay, feeling disgraced after Kutusov's appointment, wanted only to die. He rode to the fiercest fighting: yet he survived. Another officer rode even further forward, dismounted, and calmly announced he would have his breakfast. His servants laid his meal as the battle raged around him.

Below French cavalry charge to attack a Russian bastion at Borodino.

End of the day

The fearful conflict went on throughout the day, with the numbers of dead soaring every minute. Advancing troops could hardly move for the corpses strewn in their path; dying horses lay thrashing their legs.

Napoleon sat brooding on his chair; in silence he ate a slice of bread and drank a glass of red wine. On the slopes opposite, General Mikhail Kutusov sat astride a huge white horse, viewing the dreadful scene through his one good eye.

Prince Bagration, commander of the Russian Second Army, led his men forward in yet another counter-attack, only to be wounded with grapeshot which mashed one of his legs. He struggled for a moment to stay on his horse, but his knees could no longer grip; painfully he slipped from the saddle. He lay propped against a trench, his clothes blood-soaked, his pale face covered with black powder. Soon after, he died. His men fought on. They lunged forward with stained bayonets until they could hardly lift their weary arms. Soldiers who had lost their weapons fought to the death with bare bleeding hands. Horses were constantly dragged into line for repeated charges, until the animals were too tired to move faster than a walk.

Still neither side would break. Napoleon turned aside from the battle, a frown on his face: he knew decisive victory could not be gained against such stubborn Russian resistance.

And the sun began to slip through the billowing smoke, and evening came. A light rain began to fall. Borodino, described by Napoleon as "the most terrible of all my battles", came to an exhausted end. The shattered remains of the two armies drew apart.

Men slumped to the churned ground, utterly spent. Around them, corpses lay so close together that it was impossible to walk without treading on them. The French had lost perhaps 40,000 men, and the Russians slightly more. One Russian regiment, which had started the day with 1,300 men, now only had 99. Only 700 Russian prisoners were taken: the rest had fought to the death.

When darkness fell the maimed and dying were left where they had fallen. To the rear the Chief Surgeon of the Grand Army, J. D. Larrey, performed two hundred amputations during the night. The limbs he removed were heaped high around his gory lamp-lit table.

Camp fires were lit on the hills as regrouping signals for the various shattered units; wounded men staggered towards these flickering lights. General Kutusov sat at his own campfire and heard the fearful casualty reports from his battle-stained commanders. He planned his next move.

And before the grey light of dawn crept over the hideous battlefield, Kutusov had made up his mind. He had fought the engagement which everyone had wanted: now he could resume the retreat.

Top A confused scene as a bugler summons yet another French attack at Borodino.

Above Next morning, the wounded are removed from the battlefield where they have passed the night in agony.

45

3. Moscow

Many Russians in General Kutusov's army had expected, and even hoped, that battle would be resumed the next day. After all, they still held their original positions, and the spirit of the army remained superb despite the appalling suffering. The plan now announced seemed disastrous. Retreat would leave the gates of Moscow wide open to the French invaders: Kutusov's decision seemed a declaration of defeat.

Dejected Russian regiments began to trudge away from Borodino, still hoping Kutusov would order a defence of Moscow itself. Most of the wounded had to be left behind, and, as after Vitebsk and Smolensk, their fate was grim. Those who could, hobbled or crawled down the road after their retreating comrades, but hundreds perished by the wayside and in the near-by villages. Many were burned to death when the French set fire to the houses. Scores staggered as far as they could, and then collapsed, their tongues blackened by the heat. Enemy patrols stayed close on the Russians' heels, and a serious clash took place on 10th September. But three days later the Russian army came within sight of Moscow.

During the afternoon of the 13th Kutusov called a conference of his commanders in a near-by peasant's hovel. Moscow, he told his officers, was to be left undefended: the army would march on, past the capital.

The officers rose to their feet in outrage. Kutusov must be mad, they declared; Napoleon must not be allowed this triumph, and Russian troops could still stop him.

But Kutusov silenced them. "You fear a retreat through Moscow," he said, "but I regard it as far-

Opposite Napoleon sits at his desk in his bedroom in the Kremlin.

sighted. It will save the army. Napoleon is like a stormy torrent which we are as yet unable to stop. Moscow will be the sponge that sucks him in." How right he was to be.

Entry into Moscow

Heinrich Vossler had survived his bullet wound, and he emerged from his dressing station to be given a new mission: he would undertake patrols to the north of Moscow, and he prepared to leave the main army. "On my way I passed the Emperor. He seemed somewhat cold and aloof."

Napoleon had every reason to be depressed, and his misery would soon increase. His capture of Moscow would prove to be the bitterest victory of all.

The Grand Army moved forward as fast as it could. Meanwhile the Russian army moved south from Moscow on the road to Ryazan—which would let General Kutusov and his troops find fresh provisions, and allow the Russians to outflank the French should they retreat from Moscow.

For a while, the French advance troops and Russian rearguard stood facing one another outside the capital. A long stream of carriages and handcarts wound southwards. Citizens wept aloud. Babies were trundled away in wheelbarrows. Crowds milled upon the road as they sought to escape from the French, carrying their household belongings on their backs. Behind the refugees wisps of smoke began to rise from Moscow's spires and onion-shaped domes.

On 14th September the main French forces moved in. The centre of the capital now lay deathly quiet, and the French cavalry trotted through the streets with only the clatter of their horses' hooves on the cobbles to break the eerie silence. Napoleon planned to enter the city in triumph the following day. In the evening the first reports reached him of the fires spreading in the streets. During the night the wind rose to fan the flames, and the moaning of the wind was accom-

Below Napoleon and his staff watch Moscow burn from the terrace of the Kremlin.

panied by crackling and roaring as more fires broke out. At three o'clock on the night of the 15th Napoleon was awoken and told that the heart of Moscow was ablaze.

By morning, when the Emperor rode to the famous Russian palace, the Kremlin, almost half the city was in flames. Sparks jumped from one frail wooden building to another; and that night Napoleon was startled from his sleep by the smell of smoke and by the harsh glow through his window. The Emperor, who had sought such a proud entry, barely managed to get out of the Kremlin in time. The streets were choked with smoke and debris; houses were thundering to the ground on all sides, and many of the Imperial Guard perished as they hurried their leader to the Petrovsky Palace on the outskirts of Moscow.

The fire still smouldered on weeks later, with one house in two damaged or destroyed. The fire had probably been started by Cossacks as they left the city. Napoleon's victory was indeed turning to ashes.

Above The people of Moscow flee as the Cossacks set fire to their city.

Occupation

Above Arsonists caught setting fire to buildings in Moscow are executed by the French.

Napoleon based all his plans on the hope that the Russians would seek peace, now that Moscow had been occupied by his forces. Moreover, capture of this city would rekindle the spirit of his battered army.

One young lieutenant told how the troops felt when they first sighted the Russian capital. "Moscow! Moscow! was shouted in the ranks. Is that really Moscow? Yes, it is: the longed-for Moscow. A thousand voices rejoiced in the ranks. We have reached our goal. The war is coming to an end. The promised winter quarters lie before us. All difficulties, shortages, pains were forgotten."

Life seemed to be good again, despite the destruction left by the great fire. French troops swarmed over the city, and, for the first time since the invasion had begun, many slept under a roof instead of out in the open. The whole city took on the appearance of an armed camp. Troops stood their muskets in pyramids in the streets, found beds in the near-by houses, and scavenged for food and drink. "We received bread, meat, Dutch cheese, and wine in plenty. The copious meal and excellent wine worked wonders for our morale, and once again we felt proud to be soldiers of Napoleon's victorious army."

But how long would the men remain proud? And was the army really victorious? Already, the troops had begun to disgrace themselves by robbing Russian homes and even the churches. This looting went on more or less unchecked—the contents of houses were scattered over the filthy streets as men hunted and killed for any item of value.

Discipline began to collapse, as troops fought with one another for stolen property; many lay dead drunk in the gutters, empty wine and vodka bottles strewn around. Release from the tension of the march and battle had snapped the soldiers' self-control.

Now, the weather grew colder. Snow fell on the smoke-blackened ruins on 27th September, and although it melted immediately, winter lay just ahead. Napoleon's troops, equipped only for summer campaigning, looted clothing to keep them warm. According to one Russian who had stayed behind: "The French entered houses and, committing gross acts of violence, took from their owners not only money, gold and silver but even boots, linen, and—most ludicrous of all—cassocks, women's furs and cloaks, in which they stood on guard and rode on horseback. It was not uncommon for people walking in the street to be stripped to their shirt, and many were robbed of boots, overcoats, frock-coats. Anybody who resisted was beaten savagely, often to death."

The sight of Napoleon's troops dressed in women's clothes to keep out the cold summed up the difference between his army now, in September, with that which had marched so proudly over the River Niemen three months before. And the difference would soon become even more marked.

Napoleon waits

Two candles burned in Napoleon's window late every night. He worked long hours, receiving reports from Paris in a locked leather pouch with a brass plate inscribed: *The Emperor's Despatches*. He tried to improve the organization of his army's supply system. Above all, he tried to persuade the Russians to make peace.

On 20th September, two days after returning to the Kremlin when the fire died down, he wrote to Tsar Alexander at St. Petersburg. Napoleon believed his terms were generous, even though he insisted that a peace agreement must be signed in the ruins of the city he now occupied. He still felt convinced that his capture of Moscow would bring Alexander to his senses. After all, the Austrians had submitted after he had captured Vienna in 1805 and again in 1809, and the Prussians had thrown down their arms after Berlin had fallen in 1806.

But Alexander proved unexpectedly stubborn. Even if the Tsar himself had been tempted to give in, many of his advisers advised him against such an idea—especially the merchants who benefited from trade with Napoleon's other enemy, England. On 20th September, the very day Napoleon wrote his letter, the Tsar issued a proclamation to his people: "Let no one despair. Indeed, how can we lose courage when all classes of the realm are proving their courage and constancy—when the enemy finds himself with his remaining troops so far from his own country in the midst of a great nation, surrounded by our armies . . ."

Some citizens in St. Petersburg did indeed urge Alexander to seek peace. Napoleon, they claimed, might soon advance upon this second capital, and agreement should be reached before the whole of Russia was conquered.

Yet Alexander refused to listen. Day by day Napoleon hoped for a messenger from the Tsar, but none came. He repeated his offer of peace, and he also sent his *aide* Count de Lauriston to try to negotiate direct with General Kutusov. Both messengers were turned back without reaching their destinations. Napoleon sank deeper into his depression, sometimes spending hours on end without uttering a word.

On 3rd October the Emperor declared he intended to burn the remains of Moscow—fewer than five thousand houses—and then strike for St. Petersburg. His Generals were appalled: to march on this other capital would mean advancing into the bitter Russian winter. Napoleon fell silent again.

Day by day he paced his room, alone with his thoughts, and his candles continued to flicker late into the nights. He tossed in his sleep. Peace must surely come. Why did Alexander, whom he still remembered with some affection, remain so stubborn? Surely the Russians must realize that the war was lost? Why did they not behave like his other defeated opponents? The questions went unanswered. Outside the Kremlin the French troops became more and more disorganized, and the winter weather crept closer and closer.

Left Alexander I, Tsar of Russia, who refused to sue for peace and waited for Napoleon to destroy himself.

53

Napoleon decides

Above Napoleon inspects the ruins after the burning of Moscow.

Opposite Napoleon tries to shake off the burden of holding Moscow, while the Russian bears gather for the kill that they expect winter to bring.

Napoleon had made a basic mistake, fatal to any army commander. He had completely underestimated the strength of his enemy. He had no real appreciation of the Russian people and the Russian leader. The people would rather starve and die than submit to these invaders of their sacred soil. And as for Tsar Alexander, he had promised never to make peace while a single enemy soldier stood on Russian soil. He would rather eat potatoes with the peasants; and so great was the pressure put on him that he could not break his word.

So Napoleon received no answer to his offers of peace. At the start of October, he had to face three grim alternatives. First, he could advance on St. Petersburg—but this, as his generals had told him, would be almost suicidal so late in the year. Secondly, Napoleon could stay in Moscow until the spring and then advance, if the Russians still did not agree to peace.

But the Emperor always proved impatient. He could never keep still. The thought of enforced idleness during the winter months plunged him into even deeper despair. His whole energetic character cried out against the idea. Also, pressing business awaited him back home. In Spain, the English were forcing back his armies, and in Paris there were new rumours of opposition to his rule. Above all, unity in his Grand Army was fast disintegrating. This vast amalgam of nationalities, hard to control from the start, was now almost unmanageable. Only positive action would weld it together again—and besides, stocks of food and other supplies were vanishing fast.

So Napoleon came to the third and last choice: to

withdraw from Moscow. He could abandon the capital and lead his men back to Poland and neighbouring Lithuania. The troops would withdraw while the weather remained reasonable, then, after wintering on the borders of Russia, they could come back in spring to finish the campaign.

Napoleon made his decision. Once he had done so, he should have left at once: each night brought colder weather, and on 15th October three inches of snow covered the capital.

But now the French leader made another disastrous mistake. He continued to delay, still hoping for a sign from Alexander. On 18th October a sign was given, but it dashed Napoleon's last hopes: Joachim Murat suffered two and a half thousand casualties in a vicious clash with Kutusov's rearguard near the capital: the Russians were clearly still determined to fight.

That very night Napoleon issued the order to quit Moscow. To his staff he seemed unusually excited: departure would begin the following day, 19th October.

Departure

At two o'clock in the afternoon of 19th October the first men of the Grand Army began to leave Moscow. The French had occupied the capital for thirty-five days. Departure was still termed withdrawal, rather than retreat.

Napoleon's forces made a fantastic sight. Everyone was loaded down with loot: soldiers wore sheepskin jackets, fur-lined boots, fur coats—and even fur-trimmed bonnets. Their knapsacks bulged with silver and jewels, and they carted with them silks, sables, ikons, ingots, medieval suits of armour and a thousand and one useless articles—including silver chamber pots and a jewel-encrusted spittoon.

"In countless columns they moved along the broad high-road," remembered an eye-witness. "It was not only the number of fighting men who made up the endless procession, but the innumerable wagons, carts, chaises, often loaded with booty. And the number of guns, ammunition wagons, cabs, and the like, moving in eight or ten parallel columns, took up an incalculable stretch of the road."

Horsemen took to the fields wherever possible, to leave room for infantrymen and carts on the road. But still the highway became jammed. At the best, the Grand Army moved sluggishly forward, with frequent halts and bottlenecks.

The last French units left Moscow, where the charred timbers still smouldered. For four days massive explosions had torn the remains of the city: on 21st October the Kremlin itself was blown up in a last act of vandalism.

Napoleon strove to create order from his shambles of an army. He ordered that every vehicle not essential for carrying provisions should be burned, and the horses used to pull the guns instead. But his commands were disobeyed. According to a Frenchman, "Whereas most officers owned one cart, the generals had half a dozen."

And so the loot-laden vehicles continued to clog the route for withdrawal. Harnesses snapped; sands, marshes, steep hills caused delays. The army took six days to cover eighty miles. More than twelve hours were needed to travel the distance that one vehicle on its own would have done in a mere two. Yet the withdrawal should have been as fast as possible, to steal away from the waiting Russians and to escape before the foul weather took the army in its grip.

The day of departure, 19th October, had been a bright autumn day. But then came renewed rain; muddy bogs on the deplorable road made progress even slower. Men cursed as they hauled their guns and carts through the sucking mire. Napoleon set out from Moscow with 90,000 infantry, 15,000 cavalry, 569 cannon and 10,000 wagons. His army had food for twenty days, and horse fodder for less than a week.

The journey home stretched five hundred terrible miles ahead.

Below French soldiers huddle into improvised winter clothing as they begin the retreat from Moscow.

Boney Hatching a Bulletin or Snug Winter Quarters!!!

4. Retreat

Napoleon has been strongly condemned for the route he chose for withdrawal—back the same way he had come. This, say some historians, invited disaster: Napoleon should have chosen another road further south or in the north, untouched by war, where he

Above Although Napoleon now knew the desperate state his army was in, he had to send cheerful bulletins to the people of France to counter the threat of a rebellion.

58

could have found more supplies for his army.

These critics are wrong. To the south lay the main Russian army, under Mikhail Kutusov. Napoleon would have faced a full-scale battle, which he could ill afford with his army in its present shambles. In any case, the southern and northern provinces would be of little value: the Russians would burn their stores before he could seize them. In addition, Napoleon had ordered supply depots to be built along the route he had taken to reach Moscow, and he had left behind men to guard these vital dumps. His army would be able to refuel at important points such as Smolensk and Vilna—or so Napoleon believed.

And so Smolensk became Napoleon's first objective. Yet he decided against the direct route from Moscow. If he had used this stretch of road, subject to most destruction during the outwards advance, General Kutusov could have reached Smolensk before him.

But if Napoleon first made a detour south towards Kaluga, he might be able to manoeuvre the Russians back and gain valuable time. Kutusov would believe he meant to go even further south, then Napoleon would suddenly switch north-west towards Smolensk. He might even lead Kutusov into making a disastrous mistake. Besides, Kaluga contained Russian stores which the French might be able to capture. Above all, this bold threat to the Russians appealed to Napoleon's bravado

And so, after much deliberation, Napoleon had chosen his route: south to Kaluga, then westwards to Smolensk to join his previous route into Russia. He refused to listen to those who warned him that local peasants promised a bad winter. "Bah!" he replied. "You and your natives! See how fine it is . . ."

Switch to retreat

The one-eyed General Kutusov had lost none of his cunning. During the Russian retreat to Moscow, he had been urged to give battle to stop the French advance. Now, he was being pressed to fight a battle to stop the French withdrawal. But he was just as reluctant to engage the enemy.

He planned to stand back and watch the Grand Army die. Even if the French managed to survive starvation and the horrors of the Russian winter, he would still not be greatly concerned—as long as the enemy fled from Russia. This, he believed, was the main thing.

So, when French forces fought with Russian troops outside the town of Maloyaroslavets on 24th October, Kutusov refused to send in reinforcements. Instead, he went round the town and took up positions on the road to Kaluga. He watched as the houses burned and streets changed hands again and again, and eventually the French prised the Russians from their defences. Kutusov merely withdrew further down the highway to Kaluga. Then he waited.

And Napoleon, as Kutusov expected and hoped, refused to take up the challenge. The Emperor still felt too weak to risk a full-scale clash with the main Russian army. Yet only a battle would force Kutusov to stop blocking the road to Kaluga. So Napoleon had to turn away.

The French leader had failed in his bid to out-manoeuvre Kutusov. Instead of marching westwards towards Smolensk from Kaluga, he must now hurry north to rejoin the route to this city at a point nearer to Moscow than he had intended. His strike south had merely sapped his resources still further, had used up precious time—and winter loomed nearer.

Below Cossacks massacre a party of Frenchmen who have been cut off from their regiment.

Napoleon himself barely managed to avoid death on 25th October. At 7.30 in the morning he had left his thatched hut where he had spent the night, to view the Maloyaroslavets position. And as he rode towards the town, Cossack horsemen burst from a near-by wood. Down they swooped on Napoleon and his small bodyguard. An officer led cavalrymen against them, only to fall screaming as a Cossack lance skewered his horse. Another officer fought till his sword was dashed from his hand, then he flung himself on a yelling Cossack, pulling him off his horse, and the struggle continued among the pounding hooves. The enemy swirled towards Napoleon, who sat with drawn sword ready to fight to the end. But then the Cossacks spied undefended French carts. Lured by the chance of loot, they jerked round their horses and galloped away—unaware that the great Napoleon himself had almost been at their mercy.

So Napoleon survived, but only to witness the hell which his army now had to endure. Planned withdrawal was giving way to headlong retreat.

Above Even in retreat, Napoleon cut an impressive figure at the head of his army.

61

Back to Borodino

Heinrich Vossler had been detached from the main army while Napoleon had occupied Moscow, and had stayed with garrison troops near Mozhaisk. To Mozhaisk now streamed the rest of the Grand Army.

Behind them came the Russians, with Kutusov pushing forward as fast as the French—not to seek battle, but to keep the enemy on the move. And his policy now began to reap terrible rewards. The path of the armies was littered with burning villages—and strewn along the roadside were increasing numbers of stiffened bodies. Constant pressure upon the French army forced it to abandon baggage, guns, sick, wounded and loot. One by one the items were cast aside which had been plundered with so much glee in Moscow. Winter had still to come. At this stage of the retreat, hunger claimed most victims. Food supplies had already run out, with fearful consequences. First, horses were eaten. Then, the troops began to eat their dead comrades—a common practice even before Smolensk was reached.

Russian peasants were told to lure French troops from the columns by offering food and drink. Then, when their victims were drunk, they were murdered and their bodies stripped naked. An English observer, Sir Robert Wilson, saw "sixty naked men, whose necks were laid upon a felled tree, while Russian men and women with large faggot-sticks, singing in chorus and hopping around, with repeated blows struck out their brains."

Later he witnessed "a group of wounded men, at the ashes of another cottage, sitting and lying over the body of a comrade which they had roasted, and the flesh of which they had begun to eat." At one village,

Selino, a detachment of fifty French were seized by peasants and buried alive in a huge pit. A teenage drummer boy bravely led the way into this gaping grave.

Cossack horsemen were always waiting. "We had them swarming around us constantly," wrote Heinrich, "and officers or men on their own, even if they strayed no more than a hundred yards from the main body, paid for their carelessness with their lives."

Near Mozhaisk regiments in the fleeing Grand Army came upon a special horror. The French found themselves on an undulating plain, surrounded by rounded hills, covered with rotting remains of horses and corpses half-eaten by wolves, littered with broken weapons, rusty sabres, overturned guns. At first the French did not recognize the place: then they realized they were stumbling across the ghostly battlefield of Borodino.

They turned on to the road they had used to reach Moscow. Back they would go, the way they had come. And in addition to gnawing hunger, they now had to contend with agonizing cold.

Below Women and even tiny babies had been taken with the army into Russia, and perhaps they suffered worst of all during the retreat.

Winter begins

The wind shrieked from the stark pine forests. The frosty ground rang sharp beneath the horses' hooves and rumbling carts. Nightly the temperature plummeted: during darkness on 6th November the troops had to suffer twenty-two degrees of frost. Skies dulled to a deeper shade of grey. "Snow fell in enormous flakes," wrote one Frenchman. "We lost sight of the sky and the men in front of us."

Napoleon's troops still had their fur coats, stolen from the people of Moscow. But they had no protection for their faces and hands, nor for their feet when their boots wore through. Their lips cracked open and the blood froze on their chins; moisture in their nostrils turned into ice and they could barely breathe. Their noses and ears were frostbitten, turning first purple, then black, and before then the skin itself died; eventually the ears, noses or fingers would rot away and snap off like dried twigs.

"I saw a dead man," wrote one horrified Russian officer, "his teeth deep in the haunch of a horse which was still quivering. I saw a dead man inside a horse which he had disembowelled and emptied in order to crawl inside and get warm. I saw another man tearing with his teeth at the entrails of a dead horse."

Dogs which had so far managed to avoid being eaten, ate the fallen bodies of their masters. An eye-witness saw them "tearing the still living flesh from the feet, hands and limbs of moaning wretches who could not defend themselves, and whose torment was still greater, as in many cases their consciousness and senses remained."

Russian pressure eased slightly after a hard action at Dorogobuzh on 3rd November. Yet by this time,

with the cold still to become far greater, the Grand Army had already lost a third of the men, dead and captured, who had left Moscow less than three weeks before. Many of the survivors were unfit to fight: Napoleon had only about 55,000 men under his direct command who were still capable of service.

Also at Dorogobuzh, Napoleon received further unsettling news. Back in Paris, a half-mad General named Claude de Malet had tried to seize power. Malet's bid had failed, but the incident underlined the weakness of Napoleon's authority: he must get home as soon as possible. Meanwhile he spurred his tattered troops on with the promise that their ordeal would soon be over. Supplies lay ahead, he claimed. "Your hunger will finish at Smolensk."

And so the soldiers struggled on, phantoms in the swirling blizzards. They tried to ease their aching stomachs with the thought of food at Smolensk. But soon would come shattering disappointment, and the realization that the horrors had only just begun.

Above A scene from a modern Russian film about the French retreat.

Smolensk

Heinrich Vossler was among those who staggered into Smolensk, prodded on by the promise of food. "We had been told that in Smolensk we could find provisions in plenty and, what we needed just as urgently, a corps of forty thousand fresh troops. We were to be cruelly disappointed."

Napoleon had reached the city on 9th November. His original plan had been to stay in the area until spring; his troops would meanwhile live on the food which had been stocked in the city.

But Napoleon and his men found totally insufficient supplies. Little had reached the city from France and Prussia—Cossack raiding parties had wrought havoc on the convoys. And officials at Smolensk had sold some of the food which did arrive to local Jewish merchants, who had resold it to the Russians. Warehouses contained some bread, flour, salt and spirits, but the supply system had collapsed. All stocks were used up within three days: those troops who arrived later received nothing.

And the city itself, burned to a shell during the battle on the outward march, now offered no protection either from the Russians or the weather. The houses were stripped of all burnable contents, and the men made huge fires in an attempt to warm themselves, but soon all fuel would be finished, and by now snow fell almost daily. Troops in the city fell into complete chaos, fighting amongst themselves for scraps of clothing or food.

Napoleon fretted over his torn and travel-stained maps. Mikhail Kutusov lurked to the south, following a parallel route to the French; ahead, Russian forces under Prince Ludwig Wittgenstein were pushing down from the north, while others under Admiral Pavel Chichagov were moving up from the south. Napoleon risked being trapped before he could safely cross the next major obstacle, the Berezina River.

Clearly, no time could be wasted. The Emperor merely stayed at Smolensk while about fifty thousand men gathered at the city; on 14th November he led his regiments into the snowy wilderness again.

For a while even Napoleon travelled on foot, carrying a birch staff and wearing on his head a red velvet hood covered with a fur cap. After him and his Guard came the 4th Corps, led by Prince Eugène, then the 1st Corps under Davoût, and with Ney bringing up the rear.

Another corps, commanded by Marshal Victor moved further north, to hold off Wittgenstein, while Oudinot led another corps south to prevent Admiral Chichagov seizing the key bridge across the Berezina at Borissov. All thoughts of victory had long since gone; now Napoleon could hope only to survive, and at any moment Kutusov might send detachments forward to block his route.

Opposite General Ludwig Wittgenstein, a German professional soldier who served in the Russian army.

Below Napoleon returns to Smolensk as the Grand Army struggles across the plains behind him.

Krasnyi

Soon after Smolensk, Napoleon summoned enough strength at least to snarl at the enemy. He needed to gain time for Eugène, Davoût and Ney to come up closer, and to do this he would have to snap at Kutusov's lurking forces—some of whom were already blocking the road to be used by the remaining French corps.

So, on 17th November, Napoleon struck at the Russian centre at Krasnyi, using the troops of the Imperial Guard: these men had been pampered in comparison to other units, and had so far not been committed to battle.

They now fought with extreme bravery, and Napoleon managed them with his previous brilliance. The Russians were checked and drew back: Kutusov still declined to enter into all-out battle. Eugène and Davoût were able to move up, past Russian troops, to join Napoleon.

But Ney still remained behind, in territory given up to the enemy. And Napoleon had to press forward for the River Berezina, with terrible consequences for the corps he had to abandon. Ney had left Smolensk on 17th November in command of the French rearguard, together with about 8,000 wounded and women. His actual fighting strength totalled 7,000 infantrymen and 450 cavalry. Just before the Dnieper River he found himself surrounded by Russian forces under General Mikhail Miloradovich. He refused a summons to surrender and vicious fighting broke out on the ice-rutted road. Half his men were slaughtered; Ney and the survivors were forced to leave the road and take to the woods in a desperate bid to escape.

The French general led about three thousand men through the forests, making for the River Dnieper, which Ney believed would be covered in ice and so possible to cross. On they stumbled through the thigh-deep snow, floundering in the drifts, half-dead with exhaustion. One after another the Frenchmen collapsed, crawled a few more yards, then lay still. Survivors staggered on, sobbing for breath; and through the trees on either side moved the Cossacks, and the French could hear their battle-call—"a dull cry like the wind in the pines"—"*Houra, houra, houra . . .*"

At last the trees thinned, and the French emerged onto the bank of the Dnieper. On the river lay the first thin ice of winter: Ney stepped onto the surface first, and it creaked but held. Others followed.

And under the weight of the advance the ice splintered and cracked and scores plunged through to drown in the freezing water. Only Ney and eight hundred of his troops reached the far side, to rejoin the main body at Orsha. Some of his survivors had been sent mad by fear; more than fourteen thousand people, including the wounded and women, had been slaughtered by the merciless enemy.

Left Three Russian soldiers are shown removing the angelic mask from the devilish face of Napoleon's reputation.

Russian agony

But the Russians, too, were suffering. They also had to endure the atrocious conditions, and their losses were mounting daily.

Although the troops under General Kutusov and the other Russian commanders were better equipped to withstand the cold, they probably had even less food than their enemy during the second half of the French retreat. Advancing behind the French, they found that every scrap had been devoured by Napoleon's men in their frantic search for survival. Moreover, the need to keep close to the enemy meant that supplies could not be brought up quickly enough. And the Russians, like the French, suffered sheer exhaustion.

So, in six terrible weeks, the main Russian army lost over fifty thousand troops through death and desertion, and Kutusov now had fewer than thirty-five thousand fit to fight. "Each day provided fresh agony," wrote a Russian infantryman. "Our clothing had worn out. We wound cloth around our feet when our boots split, but soon these strips became blood-stained. We chewed leather to give us nourishment." He continued: "Even though the sun rarely shone, the snow glared white. Our eyes were blinded by this harsh light, sometimes for ever. Men stumbled on with their hand on the shoulder of the comrade in front. We hardly looked like a conquering army, nor did we feel like one."

Men deserted, sick and exhausted, and made their way back home: they could see no reason for further pursuit—surely the French were beaten?

Yet Kutusov was still being urged to fight a battle. Back amid the comforts of St. Petersburg, where wealthy citizens enjoyed luxurious balls, dancing beneath sparkling chandeliers, Tsar Alexander's courtiers demanded the total destruction of the enemy. Russia must be avenged.

Courier after courier reached Kutusov's headquarters with letters from the Tsar pressing for battle and urging faster pursuit. Yet the army commander knew it would be virtually impossible to quicken the pace: his forces would collapse under the extra strain. Moreover, his plan was working: the Grand Army was approaching its horrible end, even without further full-scale conflict.

Ahead, though, lay the River Berezina. This obstacle would provide the perfect setting for a trap: if the French could be blocked at the river, and the bridge at Borissov blown up, the Russian armies could converge for the final annihilation. Kutusov, whether he liked it or not, might find himself in battle.

All eyes, in St. Petersburg, in the Russian armies in the field, in the remains of the Grand Army, became fixed on this thin line on the map—the wide and fast-flowing Berezina.

Below Soldiers in the Russian winter had to cope with constant blizzards in which they could scarcely see or move.

5. Destruction

News of the French disaster had reached all the capitals of Europe. Messengers spurred their horses across the roads of Poland, Prussia, Holland, France; fast frigates unfurled their sails to take latest reports to England and even across the Atlantic to America. The whole western world watched the death agony of the Grand Army.

In faraway Spain, the Duke of Wellington rested his men at winter quarters, and the news encouraged him as he prepared for his final campaign to drive the French out of the peninsula.

In London, the Prime Minister Lord Liverpool eagerly ripped open the despatches from St. Petersburg: at last the long struggle with the French might be coming to an end. After twenty weary years, surely even Napoleon would not be able to rise again from such a defeat.

And in Berlin the Prussian monarch, Friedrich Wilhelm, began to consider tearing up his alliance with Napoleon. So far he had been intimidated by the French Emperor, ever since his armies had been crushed at Jena and Auerstädt in 1806. But now might be the time to restore Prussia's battered military honour and raise her once-proud eagle standards high again.

Reports were awaited with most impatience in Napoleon's own capital. The recent attempt by General Claude de Malet to seize power in Paris had fed the unease already felt by Napoleon's supporters: although news of the fate of the Grand Army was severely censored before reaching the ordinary people, opposition to Napoleon might now be expected to grow.

So, for a multitude of reasons, events in Russia had tremendous importance for politicians, generals and men and women in all European countries. An era might be coming to an end as the remains of the Grand Army dragged themselves towards Berezina, leaving a bloody trail across the Russian snow.

Above The Duke of Wellington, the British general who was slowly destroying Napoleon's power in Spain and Portugal.

Towards the Berezina

On the outward journey towards Moscow, the River Berezina had seemed harmless enough, quietly flowing between green banks. The troops had hardly noticed the crossing. Now the name Berezina was to become a symbol of hell on earth.

Napoleon pushed his men forward as fast as he could to reach the river before the Russians could close their trap. He had fewer than 40,000 men still capable of fighting, and thousands of these were of doubtful value. Against him, Chichagov was rushing 25,000 men towards the far bank of the Berezina, while Prince Ludwig Wittgenstein, with 35,000, would thrust down from the north on Napoleon's side of the river.

Kutusov, with 35,000 troops now directly in Napoleon's rear, seemed in a perfect position for the final blow. But the Russian commander remained cautious. His own troops were nearing total exhaustion; Wittgenstein was believed to have an obsessive fear of Napoleon, and Pavel Chichagov was a sailor, not a soldier.

Yet on 16th November Admiral Chichagov's vanguard occupied Minsk and pushed towards Borissov on the Berezina. Only the day before, Wittgenstein had clashed with French troops under Marshal Victor, pushed north by Napoleon in an attempt to gain time for the rest of the army to make the crossing at Borissov.

But Tsar Alexander ordered Wittgenstein to deal not only with Victor, but also with Oudinot, by throwing him back before he could stop Chichagov's advance. This meddling by Alexander gave Napoleon a glimmer of hope. Oudinot had advanced rapidly

Below A French officer surveys his dejected troops.

74

BEREZINA

Artillery
Prussian Fire Positions
French Fire Positions

0   ½   1
scale in miles

towards the vital bridge over the Berezina at Borissov, and although his troops were unable to stop Chichagov's men from burning this bridge, they had beaten back the Admiral's regiments.

Wittgenstein could not possibly deal with both Victor and Oudinot, as instructed by Alexander, because they lay too far apart. And in trying to do both, he did neither properly. Victor managed to pull back to join Napoleon, and the Russian regiments under Wittgenstein could not reach Oudinot's corps in time.

Here Napoleon showed his genius. The enemy were temporarily off-balance, with Admiral Chichagov reeling back and Wittgenstein making a difficult cross-country move. Kutusov lay behind, but perhaps two days' march or more away. Napoleon had been given some grace, if only a matter of hours, and now the Emperor seized his chance.

On 23rd November, the forward French patrols emerged from the black woods to see before them a wide expanse of brown muddy water, with ice whirling in the fast currents—the Berezina. The bridge at Borissov had been destroyed; the Grand Army seemed trapped. But Napoleon had made his plan.

Berezina bridges

Napoleon reached the river late in the afternoon, 25th November. He knew he must now be outnumbered three to one; he had to find a way across this barrier before the enemy could unleash their united forces upon him. Calmly, he put his plan into action.

Scouts had already been sent ahead to study the area. And according to a local peasant, an unmarked ford stretched across the river nine miles to the north, near the village of Studienka. The water swirled too deep for the ford to be used—but the depth at this point might not be too great for bridges.

Napoleon still had the necessary equipment, carefully carried from Smolensk for this purpose: two field forges, two wagons of charcoal for fuel, and six of engineering tools. Houses could be demolished for timber; his engineers had slogged through the snow, humping thousands of nails in their haversacks.

But the Russians must be fended off while the rough bridges could be built. By a number of feints Napoleon therefore fixed enemy attention on Borissov, rather than Studienka, and to confuse the enemy still further, he sent a detachment six miles downstream to fell trees noisily, as if a bridge were about to be built there. The trick worked: Chichagov scurried southwards to this spot. "I've duped the Admiral," declared Napoleon with delight.

Wearing a grey overcoat, the Emperor watched his men on the 26th as they slaved up to their armpits in icy water. They worked for twenty-four hours with only brief rests, when Napoleon had wine issued to them, and at the end of this time they had constructed the two crossings: a light bridge for infantry, and a heavier one two hundred yards downstream for wagons and cannon. Napoleon stepped onto the fresh planks, nailed across the trestles driven into the mud. He stamped his boot and heard the solid thud. "Excellent!" he exclaimed.

Behind him in the woods and snowy wastes the surviving regiments of the Grand Army anxiously waited. Cossacks still hovered around the depleted French units. The main Russian armies would soon arrive: already Chichagov had realized his blunder and was hurrying troops northwards to the far bank again.

Napoleon had given orders that the fighting men should cross first; then, if time remained, the hordes of unarmed French, the wounded, sick, women and children would follow. If there was no time for these non-combatants, the bridges would be blown: those still to cross would be left at the mercy of the Cossacks.

Nicolas Oudinot would lead the first troops. This French commander's favourite game was shooting out candles with his pistols after dinner; he had thirty wounds on his body to show his battle experience. Now he had the honour of forcing the path across the Berezina.

Below The French army comes under fire from Russian artillery as they begin to cross the Berezina.

Berezina crossing

Oudinot clattered across the frail wooden life-line with eleven thouand men, while engineers put the finishing touches to the heavier bridge. At 4 p.m. on the 26th Napoleon began sending guns, wagons and cavalry across this second structure.

On the far bank Oudinot had clashed fiercely with Chichagov's regrouping forces. Up to thirty thousand Russians were now hammering at the French troops who had crossed the river: Oudinot himself was shot out of his saddle, and although he survived his wounds, Ney had to take over his command.

This struggle by Oudinot and Ney and their men ranks amongst the bravest of the whole campaign. Time and again the Russians tried to batter them back into the river. The woods echoed with screams, crackling muskets, belching cannons and pounding

Above The scene of utter chaos as the retreating French fight each other to reach the two improvised bridges across the Berezina.

cavalry charges; smoke swirled high in the snowy air. But the French clung to the far bank, holding back the Russians to enable more men to cross the Berezina behind them.

All that night and next day, 27th November, weary regiments flooded over the bridges. Napoleon himself crossed with his Guard at 2 p.m. on the 27th. Numbers on the western bank swelled; gradually Admiral Chichagov's men fell back.

A captain in the Imperial Guard described his crossing. First he and his men had to force their way through the disorganized crowd on the eastern bank—soon this mob would reach tragic proportions. "In the end we drew our swords and behaved like madmen, using the flat of the blade to knock aside those who, pushed back by the crowd, hemmed us in as if in a press . . . On reaching the bridge to which we had been directed, we began to dismount and cross one by one, leading our horses so as not to shake the bridge. It had no guard-rail, was almost at water-level, covered by a layer of manure, and was already seriously damaged, dislocated, sagging in places, and unsteady everywhere."

Engineers plunged into the freezing water to repair the trestles, and the structures still held. Many of those workmen perished through the cold. But the French regiments continued to cross, one by one, until Napoleon had brought most of his fighting strength to the other side. He had almost achieved the impossible.

Yet Marshal Victor's corps had still to come over, together with thousands of stragglers, wounded, and women and families who had accompanied the army. Amongst the men remaining on the threatened bank was Heinrich Vossler. And now a fresh horror arrived, more dreadful than any so far in the 1812 campaign.

Death at the bridges

"This day, and the cruel spectacle of it all, is something I shall never forget as long as I live." So wrote Lieutenant Vossler, describing his experiences of 28th November.

Heinrich Vossler had been with Victor's corps, ordered to ward off Prince Ludwig Wittgenstein who had now reached the eastern bank of the Berezina. Late on the 27th the Russian guns had opened up on the remnants of the Grand Army still struggling to cross, and Cossacks had begun to knife into the rabble around the bridges. The attacks were intensified on the 28th, and about twenty-five thousand people had still to step on to the bridges: for some inexplicable reason the crossings had been stopped during the previous night.

Marshal Victor's corps tried to block the Russians as long as possible; then Heinrich and his comrades made for the bridges. Heinrich had started for the area at three o'clock in the morning, to be one of the first to cross at daybreak—but he was still struggling to reach the structures at midday.

Confusion had now reached an appalling level. Early on the 28th the heavier bridge collapsed, and although frantic efforts were made to repair it, by noon it had become totally unusable. "An immense flood of men, horses and wagons now surged towards the other bridge," wrote Heinrich. "In the frightful crush men and horses were squeezed and trampled underfoot in their hundreds. The bridge was so narrow that it could only take two or three men abreast."

Only the previous day Heinrich had blessed the fact that the temperature had risen, but now the blessing

became a curse: the rise had caused a thaw which had skimmed the ice off the water. The air grew cold again, but the ice remained too thin to walk on, while the water was too cold for attempts to swim: many tried, and perished in the currents.

Others waded out and tried to clamber on the bridge further from the bank, but as they grasped the wood their hands were hacked and severed by those struggling to cross. Crowds pressing from behind forced dozens of those on the bridge into the water, and this pressure increased tenfold when the shriek came from the rear: "Cossacks are coming!"

Heinrich wrote: "The fight for a passage reached its ultimate horror when the Russian guns began to find the range of the milling mass, spreading death and destruction. From now on it was a fight of each man against his neighbour. The stronger trampled their weaker comrades to the ground . . ."

Shells screamed into the packed mob. The Cossacks scythed in from behind with their blood-chilling yell: "*Houra! Houra!*" Sobbing men and women clawed their way over corpses and fallen friends, and in the midst of them struggled Heinrich.

Above One of the bridges collapses, throwing people and horses into the icy river.

Flight of Napoleon

Above Claude Malet, the French general who tried to stir up a rebellion while Napoleon was in Russia.

Heinrich found himself hurled to the ground and he lay pinned beneath his horse while the rabble swirled around and over him. "I was about to resign myself to my fate."

And then he received help from a fellow-German, a cavalryman, who hauled him and his horse to their feet. "With his huge, powerful horse he pressed ruthlessly on, riding down whatever could not get out of his way in time, and I followed in his wake. By an almost superhuman effort we reached the bank."

Their first desperate attempt to clamber on the bridge failed. Then they made it, and Heinrich found himself washed across in the tide of men pushing along the reddened shaking planks. He reached the far side and safety, weeping with relief. He waited for the cavalryman who had saved his life—but he never saw his saviour again.

And, at nine o'clock on the morning of the 29th French engineers destroyed the remaining bridge, despite the indescribable cries from those still stranded. The Russians swarmed in among them. Trampled by horses, slaughtered by cannon-fire or slashing sabres, frozen to the ground, the victims were stripped by the Cossacks and tossed in the filthy snow.

Acres of ground were strewn with mutilated bodies and the shrieking wounded. The massacre went on until few remained alive. The total deaths could never be calculated, but perhaps amounted to twenty thousand. And although the bulk of the fighting units of the Grand Army had been led to the far bank by Napoleon, half would die on the next stretch of the retreat between the Berezina and Vilna.

Napoleon did not witness the death throes of his

army. Five days after the river crossing he called a Council of War. For the first time he told his Generals about the attempted takeover of power in Paris on 22nd October, led by General Malet. Further reports of unrest had arrived.

The Generals agreed with Napoleon that he himself ought to be in the French capital when the full news reached home of the disaster suffered by the Grand Army. Besides, Napoleon could do nothing more in Russia: ahead lay Vilna where food would be stored. Until then, no man could help the surviving soldiers: every man must help himself.

Napoleon therefore handed over command to Marshal Joachim Murat, and left the army at 10 p.m. on 5th December. His commanders had tears in their eyes as they watched him go. He travelled on in a horse-drawn sleigh, shivering despite his furs, woollen clothing and heavy bearskin boots.

Below Napoleon, in disguise, dashing back from Russia to put down Malet's rising.

Last days

Even more than before, it was bad weather and hunger, rather than the Russians, that slaughtered the French during the last miles of the march; indeed, the Russians suffered almost as much as their prey.

Cold and fearful hunger, the enemies of both sides, often brought men from each army together. They huddled around the same roadside fires, and heaped the corpses of dead soldiers about them to provide protection from the icy gales. But other Russian soldiers, and especially the Cossacks, kept up their relentless attacks.

Vilna did indeed contain food. Like crazed animals, the half dead troops crammed it into their mouths. Many died with the sudden end to starvation. "I saw terrifying corpses in the streets," wrote a French lady, "seated on the ground, leaning against walls, preserved by the cold, their limbs shrunken and stiff in the position in which Death had overtaken them."

Of those who survived these last days of the retreat, thousands lost hands, feet, noses and ears from the frost. After the Berezina and before Morodochno the temperature never rose above twenty-six degrees below zero. When the French stumbled into Vilna, the temperature fell to nearly forty degrees below.

Heinrich Vossler emerged physically unscathed, except for a blotched complexion which would stay with him always; but mentally he had been changed for life: the nightmare retreat would haunt him forever. He had seen men die in agony, one after the other in an endless stream. He had seen men sinking their teeth into human corpses in an effort to survive. He wrote: "It was not unknown even for men to gnaw

at their own famished bodies." Many men went mad during the retreat. Most lapsed into deep lethargy, known as "the Moscow depression."

Groups of men crawled onwards through Vilna and along the road to the Niemen—the river which they had crossed with so much hope and bravado six months before. At last the marauding Cossacks turned away.

The first survivors reached the Niemen on 14th December, watched with growing horror by the French units which had been left to guard the river. Count Louis Philippe de Segur, on Murat's staff, gave this terrible description: "Instead of the 400,000 companions who had fought so many successful battles with them, who had swept so masterfully into Russia, they saw emerging from the white, ice-bound wilderness only 1,000 infantrymen and troopers under arms, nine cannon, and 20,000 stragglers dressed in rags, with bowed heads, dull eyes, ashen, cadaverous faces and long, ice-stiffened beards. This was the Grand Army . . ."

Above The battered remnants of the Grand Army stagger back into Paris a year after their departure.

85

Death of an army

Above Napoleon, still in disguise, asks the way to the French Embassy at a house in Dresden, in Saxony.

About nine men in ten in the Grand Army died, or proved too weak or wounded to be of any further use as soldiers. Never before, and never since, has an army suffered such colossal casualties.

As many as 160,000 horses and 1,000 guns were also left behind. One *aide-de-camp* lost 17 horses during the campaign. Out of 1,100 cavalrymen the 7th Hussars could only muster 120 when the retreat ended, and only 20 were mounted. General Louis-Henri Loison, whose troops were among the first to reach safety, lost 12,000 of his 15,000 men, most of them in the space of three days.

Russian losses were also stupendous. Perhaps as many as 200,000 died, and almost three-quarters of the survivors had been seriously affected by frost-bite.

Facts and figures are endless. All add up to a tragic tale of unprecedented horror and misery, which it is hard to imagine. And these statistics underline the central theme: most of the killed and injured suffered from the weather and hunger, not the direct actions of the enemy.

Yet the winter of 1812 was no more severe than usual. Stories that the bad weather started earlier than usual are untrue. Instead, both armies were unprepared, especially the French. And this lack of preparation forms the biggest reason for Napoleon's ghastly failure.

Napoleon pondered his mistakes on his long sleigh-ride from Russia. He believed he had made two serious errors. The first had been back in July, when he had "thought to obtain in one year what could only be gained by two campaigns." He should have stayed at Vitebsk instead of venturing further into

Russia to seek battle; the Russians would probably have opened peace negotiations, claimed Napoleon. "By now Alexander would have been on his knees to me."

Secondly, Napoleon admitted he should have left Moscow sooner. He had stayed a fortnight too long, and so could not escape before the rough winter weather overtook him. "I thought that I should be able to make peace, and that the Russians were anxious for it. I was deceived and I deceived myself."

Napoleon gave no credit to the Russians for what had happened. Nor did they really deserve it. From the start the Russian generals had argued over the plan of campaign, and most of their ideas would have been disastrous if they had been accepted. And the only reason why they were not adopted was because the generals continued to squabble.

In the end, through circumstances rather than planning, the Russians had taken the best step—to keep withdrawing. Only General Kutusov displayed real wisdom, yet the central theme still holds true: Russia's victory came through Napoleon's mistakes, and through the winter weather over which they had no control.

Below Napoleon crosses the Elbe on his return to France.

Legacy

This appalling catastrophe was to dog Napoleon Bonaparte for the rest of his career. War continued, and Napoleon even managed to scrape together a new army. By April 1813, he could move on to the offensive again in Germany with a force of two hundred thousand. But these troops, gathered and equipped so quickly, were woefully inexperienced, and his new army was especially weak in cavalry.

Lack of equipment and experience would hamper Napoleon's forces during the convulsive campaigns of 1813 and 1814. Moreover, the French Emperor had now to fight against an overwhelming enemy array: in January, 1813, the Prussians tore up their French alliance and joined the Russians, Swedes, British and later the Austrians to oppose France.

Despite superb generalship, even Napoleon could not succeed against such odds. The giant clashes of 1813, at Lutzen and Bautzen in May, Dresden in August, and the "Battle of the Nations" at Leipzig in October, combined with the British advance in the Spanish peninsula, gradually sapped French strength. The allies pressed closer to France, and in spring 1814 crossed the frontier. Paris capitulated on 31st March. Napoleon abdicated, retiring to the island of Elba. He returned the following year, scratched together yet another army—and marched to his final destruction at the Battle of Waterloo.

Paradoxically, Napoleon himself never fought with more brilliance than in 1813 and 1814. But, after the 1812 disaster in Russia, he had too little backing while his enemies had renewed strength and confidence. Borodino, Moscow and the Berezina were the first steps towards Napoleon's eventual downfall on the field of Waterloo.

Ten years after the retreat through Russia, a Prussian officer visited the site of Napoleon's two bridges across the Berezina. His harrowing words provide a fitting epitaph to the Grand Army:

"As one approached the river, melancholy relics lay thicker and even in heaps, mingled with the bones of human beings and animals, skulls, tin fittings, bandoliers, bridles, and suchlike. Scraps of the bearskins of the Guard had survived . . .

"Where the main bridge had been, an island close to the bank divides the river into two arms. This island owes its origin to the vehicles and bodies which had fallen off the bridge, and to the corpses which were carried down to this point and then covered with mud and sand . . .

"We made our way with difficulty along the bank amid relics of all kinds, and soon reached the second footbridge. Here in particular we came on piles of fittings and mountings, or what remained of them. . . . Below the island three boggy mounds had been formed, and these we found covered with forget-me-not . . ."

Below Napoleon mounts his horse to escape from the battlefield after his final defeat at Waterloo.

Table of dates

1769   Birth of Napoleon.
1789   French Revolution begins.
1796   Napoleon's successful campaign in Italy (March–May).
1797   Napoleon conquers Austria (March).
1800   Defeat of Austrians at Marengo (June).
1801   Alexander becomes Tsar of Russia.
1804   Napoleon becomes Emperor of France.
1805   Napoleon defeats Austrians and Russians at Austerlitz (December).
1806   Napoleon defeats Prussians at Jena and Auerstädt (October).
1807   Napoleon defeats Russians at Eylau and Friedland (February and June).
1809   Napoleon defeats Austrians at Wagram (July).
1812   24th June—French advance begins over River Niemen.

23rd July—clash at Mogilev.

25th July—Russian delaying action at Vitebsk.

1st August—Russian armies unite near Smolensk.

16th August—Battle of Smolensk.

18th August—French possess Smolensk.

19th August—Fighting at Valutino Gora.

7th September—Borodino.

14th September—French enter Moscow.

20th September—Napoleon makes first attempt to open peace talks.

19th October—French begin to withdraw from Moscow.

24th October—Battle of Maloyaroslavets.

3rd November—French reach Dorogobuzh.

1812   9th November—Napoleon reaches Smolensk.
        17th November—Fighting at Krasnyi.
        23rd November—French reach Berezina.
        26th–28th November—Crossing of Berezina.
        5th December—Napoleon leaves for Paris.
        14th December—First survivors emerge from
           Russian territory.

1814   Allies enter Paris (March) and Napoleon abdicates, retiring to Elba.

1815   Napoleon finally defeated at the Battle of Waterloo.

Glossary

CARABINIER Soldier armed with carbine, a short firearm originally intended for cavalry use.

CHAISE Pleasure or travelling carriage, usually four-wheeled and open.

CHASSEUR Light infantry soldier.

COMMISSARIAT Department concerned with supplies of food, etc.

CONSCRIPT Recruit obliged to join the army under the laws of his country.

COSSACK Native Russian horseman, renowned for skill in riding and cruelty in combat.

CUIRASSIER Horse soldier wearing cuirass, a form of body-armour consisting of breast and back plates fastened together.

DRAGOON Cavalryman, originally mounted infantry-man armed with carbine.

HUSSAR Soldier of light cavalry regiment.

IMPERIAL GUARD Elite French troops formed for special duties, who often guarded Napoleon himself.

UHLAN Cavalryman armed with lance.

VOLTIGEUR Light infantry soldier, usually armed with rifle rather than musket.

Above The French *cuirassiers* charging in battle. These horse soldiers wore cuirass, or body-armour made up of breast and back plates, to protect them from the gunfire and bayonet thrusts of the enemy.

Right An officer of the Imperial Guard, the élite French troops who often guarded Napoleon himself.

Further reading

Brett-James, Antony, *1812, Eyewitness Accounts of Napoleon's Defeat in Russia* (Macmillan, 1967), Exciting and well-edited collection of authentic descriptions.

Chandler, D. G., *The Campaigns of Napoleon* (London, 1967). Valuable and comprehensive source book, underlining Napoleon's genius.

Cronin, Vincent, *Napoleon* (Collins, 1971). Recent biography of the French Emperor, in which Napoleon receives sympathetic treatment.

Duffy, Christopher, *Borodino, Napoleon against Russia* (Weidenfeld and Nicolson, 1972). Careful examination of this monumental battle and events leading up to it; includes a comparison of opposing armies and weapons.

Holmes, E. R., *Borodino 1812* (Charles Knight, 1971). Concise yet detailed examination of the battle, stressing its importance.

Palmer, Alan, *Napoleon in Russia* (London, 1967). An excellent survey using a wide variety of sources.

Palmer, Alan, *Russia in War and Peace* (Weidenfeld and Nicolson, 1972). Copiously illustrated survey of the Russian background during the period 1805–1814.

Tolstoy, Leo, *War and Peace* (Penguin Classics, 1957, two volumes). The famous novel of the period, containing a classic description of Borodino and brilliantly evoking the atmosphere of the campaign.

Vossler, Heinrich, *With Napoleon in Russia, 1812* (The Folio Society, 1969). Exciting and moving eye-witness account, written by the young officer featured in this book.

Index

Picture credits

The Publishers wish to thank the following for their kind permission to reproduce copyright illustrations on the pages mentioned: J. E. Bulloz, *jacket* (front); The Mansell Collection, *jacket* (back), 26, 71; the Radio Times Hulton Picture Library, *frontispiece*, 9, 10, 11, 13, 14, 20, 24, 25, 31, 45 (bottom), 47, 49, 50, 53, 54, 55, 57, 58, 60, 61, 66, 67, 69, 81, 83, 86, 87, 89; Novosti Press Agency, 16, 28, 33, 35, 36, 37, 38, 39, 65, 74; Mary Evans Picture Library, 17, 22, 29, 42, 63, 82, 85; Musee de l'Armee, 45 (top); Reunion des Musees Nationaux, 77; Heinemann Educational Books, 21. All other illustrations are from Wayland Picture Library.